Tidbits

A Collection of Service Stories, Poems, Famous Sayings, Puns and Anecdotes

Bob LeBlanc

Tellwell Talent
www.tellwell.ca

ISBN
978-0-2288-2878-5 (Paperback)
978-0-2288-2879-2 (eBook)

A NOTE FROM THE AUTHOR

This book is a compilation of items I have treasured over the years.

A few of them are from other publications, and I have done my level best to properly acknowledge the sources. Much of this book is based on personal experiences and I have written the material accordingly.

The caricatures were expertly drawn by Kim Furey to whom I send my sincere thanks. Special thanks also to Diane Dahli for her invaluable assistance, to Lise Gyorkos for her ongoing support and expertise, to Mike Shepherd and Marc LeBlanc whose contributions were most appreciated.

An excerpt from the book *Living the Gift* is gratefully reproduced with the kind permission of Pauline Murray of Living the Gift Publications.

Enjoy!

Make a friend when you don't need one.

EDITOR VS. PUBLISHER

It is most interesting that many have no idea what the difference is between a publisher and an editor. Well, the difference is rather simple. Let us use a magazine as an example. An editor is responsible for the content of the magazine. For instance, all of the editorial content, the stories, the articles, etc. are all the responsibility of the editor. In other words, the product itself, all of its contents and all the decisions relating to the editorial phase of the magazine.

The publisher on the other hand, is responsible for everything that relates to the actual publishing of the piece. The printer (and pricing), the space of operation and the control of all costs relating to the magazine. He or she hires all staff, (including the editor), the sales team and the training and follows up on all activity relating to sales. If a receptionist is required, that person would also fall under the umbrella of the publisher.

In simple terms then, the editor looks after putting out the magazine and the publisher looks after the business end of things.

As you may have noticed in my biography, I had a career as a publisher so the difference between these two procedures is very clear to me. However, in producing this book, I had to avail myself of both of these functions in order to get the book published. My thanks to the tellwell organization who provided both these facets needed in order to publish the book.

I am yesterday, and I know tomorrow. - Reginald Fessenden

FEEL
GOOD
STORIES

A BROADWAY HIGHLIGHT

Living in Halifax permits easy access to the shows on New York's Broadway, since direct flights are available from Halifax to Newark. A short bus drive from Newark brings one to the Great White Way. One of my favourite Broadway musicals is *The Secret Garden*, an adaptation of the beloved children's novel of the same name. It happens that I have seen this production four times, three times on Broadway and once locally in Victoria.

During one of my visits to New York, I attended a production called *An Evening with Rodgers and Hammerstein* presented by a group of five singers. While reading the bios of the singers, I noted that one of the performers had actually been a member of the cast of *The Secret Garden*.

As is often the case on Broadway, there were cast members at the top of each of the two exit isles, the purpose being to promote donations for the finding of a cure for AIDS. I noted that the performer at the exit I was about to take was the one who had performed in *The Secret Garden*. I mentioned my appreciation for this show and she told me that the lady who wrote the music of this production, Lucy Simon, was there that day. She said she believed

Lucy had just gone to the ladies' washroom. When I asked how I would recognize her, she asked me if I knew what Carly Simon looked like. When I said yes, she said the sisters looked very much alike and that she would be accompanied by her petite mother.

I then stationed myself outside the washroom in question and very soon, Lucy Simon appeared. She was most appreciative of my compliments regarding the music in *The Secret Garden.* She was a very gracious lady and, given my fascination for the production, it was a magic moment for me to meet this very talented lady.

Afterwards, it occurred to me that composers don't have the opportunity to receive direct accolades the way the actors on stage do. It is a fact of life for them and accordingly, Ms. Simon was more than appreciative of me (or anyone) for recognizing and applauding her talent.

The first Broadway show I saw was *My Fair Lady* and I was hooked. Subsequently, I saw the original of *The Music Man* (twice) and to this day *Till There Was You* is one of my favourite songs. I continued my visits to Broadway over the years and was fortunate to see performances of *Les Misérables*, *The Phantom of the Opera*, *A Chorus Line* and *Guys and Dolls* among others. I became a devoted fan of Broadway especially since it was so accessible from Halifax. *The Secret Garden*, Rebecca Luker (who played the

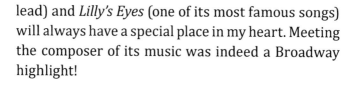

lead) and *Lilly's Eyes* (one of its most famous songs) will always have a special place in my heart. Meeting the composer of its music was indeed a Broadway highlight!

There are short cuts to happiness and dancing is one of them!

THE LAST STANDING OVATION

Kathleen was a very popular singer, pianist and organist accompanist, who passed away at the ripe old age of eighty-six. Being British (a former member of the d'Oyle Carte G&S Society), she specialized in interpreting songs by Vera Lynn. A church service with a mass was held in her honour. Many of her acquaintances and well-known performers were in attendance and delivered eulogies, not a difficult task for this lady who was very loved and respected by all.

When the service ended, one of her acquaintances appeared at the front of the church. The eulogies were properly completed by then but this gentleman had something else in mind. He asked everyone in the church to stand. In fact, he had to make the request twice.

"Since Kathleen had received many standing ovations in her lifetime, it seems appropriate that we should give her one more," he said.

Everyone then started to clap and clap and clap. It was a touching moment for all to say goodbye to a grand lady. The event concluded with all attendees singing the Vera Lynn song that Kathleen had performed so well, so many times, *We'll Meet Again*.

If plan A doesn't work, change the plan but never the goal!

LIFE'S LESSONS

As she stood in front of her fifth-grade class on the very first day of school, she told the children an untruth. Like most teachers, she looked at her students and said that she loved them all the same. However, that was impossible, because there in the front row, slumped in his seat, was a little boy named Teddy Stoddard.

Mrs. Thompson had watched Teddy the year before and noticed that he did not play well with the other children, that his clothes were messy and that he constantly needed a bath. In addition, Teddy could be unpleasant. It got to the point where Mrs. Thompson would take delight in marking his papers with a broad red pen, making bold "X"s and then putting a big "F" at the top of his papers.

At the school where Mrs. Thompson taught, she was required to review each child's past records and she put Teddy's off until last. However, when she reviewed his file, she was in for a surprise.

Teddy's first-grade teacher wrote, "Teddy is a bright child with a ready laugh. He does his work neatly and has good manners...he is a joy to be around."

His second-grade teacher wrote, "Teddy is an excellent student, well liked by his classmates, but he is troubled because his mother has a terminal illness and life at home must be a struggle."

His third-grade teacher wrote, "His mother's death has been hard on him. He tries to do his best, but his father doesn't show much interest, and his home life will soon affect him if some steps aren't taken."

Teddy's fourth-grade teacher wrote, "Teddy is withdrawn and doesn't show much interest in school. He doesn't have many friends and he sometimes sleeps in class."

Mrs. Thompson realized the problem, and she was ashamed of herself. She felt even worse when her students brought her Christmas presents wrapped in beautiful ribbons and bright paper. Teddy's present was clumsily wrapped in heavy brown paper from a grocery bag.

Mrs. Thompson took pains to open it in the middle of the other presents. Some of the children started to laugh when she found a rhinestone bracelet with some of the stones missing, and a bottle that was one-quarter full of perfume. But she stifled the children's laughter when she put the bracelet on and exclaimed how pretty it was. She then dabbed some of the perfume on her wrist. Teddy Stoddard stayed after school that day just long enough to say, "Mrs. Thompson, you smelled just like my mother used to."

After the children left, she cried for at least an hour. On that very day, she quit teaching reading, writing and arithmetic. Instead, she began to teach children and paid particular attention to Teddy. As she worked with him, his mind seemed to come alive. The more she encouraged him, the faster he responded. By the end of the year, Teddy had become one of the smartest children in the class and, despite her lie that she would love all the children the same, Teddy became one of her "teacher's pets."

A year later, she received a note from Teddy telling her she was the best teacher he had ever had. Six years went by before she got another note from Teddy. He wrote that he had finished high school, third in his class, and she was still the best teacher he had ever had in his life.

Four years after that, she got another letter saying that while things had been tough at times, he'd stayed in school, had stuck with it, and would soon graduate from college with the highest of honours. He assured Mrs. Thompson that she was still the best teacher he had ever had in his whole life.

Four more years passed and yet another letter came. This time he explained that after he got his bachelor's degree, he decided to go a little further. The letter explained that she was still the best and his most favourite teacher. But now his name was a little longer...The letter was signed, Theodore F. Stoddard, MD

The story does not end there.

There was yet another letter that spring. Teddy said that he had met this girl and was going to be married. He explained that his father had died a couple of years ago and he was wondering if Mrs. Thompson would agree to sit at the wedding in the place that was usually reserved for the mother of the groom. Of course, Mrs. Thompson did.

And guess what? She wore that bracelet, the one with several rhinestones missing. Moreover, she made sure she was wearing the perfume that Teddy remembered his mother wearing on their last Christmas together. They hugged each other, and Dr. Stoddard whispered in Mrs. Thompson's ear, "Thank you Mrs. Thompson for believing in me. Thank you so much for making me feel important and showing me that I could make a difference."

Mrs. Thompson, with tears in her eyes, whispered back. She said, "Teddy, you have it all wrong. You were the one who taught me that I could make a difference. I didn't know how to teach until I met you."

This inspirational story about Dr. Teddy Stoddard has been told on TV by Paul Harvey, Robert Schuller and many others. Dr. Wayne Dyer featured it on PBS Television. He passed away several years ago, but left the instruction "Warm someone's heart today...pass this along." That is precisely what we are doing. There is no real Teddy Stoddard. This is a fictional story written by Elizabeth Silance Stoddard in l975.

Believe in angels then return the favor. - Wayne Dyer

HOBNOBBING WITH THE HABS

While living in Moncton, NB, in the mid '60s, I was a part-time writer for the sports department of the *Moncton Times/Transcript*. Since I would be travelling to Montreal on another matter, I asked the sports editor if it was possible to arrange for a ticket to a Montreal Canadiens hockey game. As it happened, they were playing against the Chicago Blackhawks the night that I would be in Montreal. I had been (and still am to this day) a fan of the Canadiens, so this request was obviously all important to me.

The sports editor said he would send a telegram to a Mr. Camille DesRoches of the Canadiens, inquiring as to the availability of a ticket for that particular game. Mr. DesRoches replied that the writer merely had to show up at the "press" door and give his name. He then would be accommodated to see the game.

Mr. DesRoches was a prince of a gentleman and greeted me like a long-lost friend. He advised that I would be seated in the press box with the other writers, introduced me to a few of them and hoped I would enjoy the game. He even came to get me during the intermissions and took me to the writers' room where the team entertained those who were covering the game.

This was in the days of the six-team league, and the game in question would decide which team would finish first. It was a thrilling game won by the Canadiens, but the best was yet to come. After the game, Mr. DesRoches again sought me out and asked if I would like to go to the dressing room. Well, what a thrilling question! "Of course, I would!" I said. He guided me to the Habs' room where the coach, Toe Blake, was sitting on a table answering questions from reporters. Mr. DesRoches then parted the mob and said — and I remember this distinctly — "Toe, I would like you to meet Bob LeBlanc of the Moncton papers."

To say that I was enthralled by the whole situation would be a gross understatement. Here I was, a nobody from Moncton hobnobbing in the Montreal Canadiens' dressing room. I met Jean Beliveau, Henri Richard and several of the Montreal players. I was in seventh heaven! An unforgettable experience!

I subsequently lived in Montreal from 1968 to 1972 and the Forum was an important part of my life. I had season tickets and attended most of the team's home games.

The Forum undertook a complete renovation in 1968. It started in May immediately after a game (which I was fortunate to attend) and re-opened again in the fall of 1968 without missing a beat (an event I was also privileged to attend). As we left the building, I vividly recall seeing all the construction equipment waiting to begin the renovation.

Traditions associated with the Forum are numerous, from the twenty-four Stanley Cup banners hanging from the rafters, to the players' numbers that have been retired over the years. It was a unique building, and I will never forget my visit there in l965.

The old Forum, of course, is no longer used by the Montreal Canadiens since they moved to the Centre Bell in 1997. The seating capacity of both locales is the same: 17,959. In 1997, the Forum was declared a National Historic Site of Canada. It is presently a multiplex movie theatre.

Nothing is impossible to the willing mind. - Books of the Han dynasty.

I WISH YOU ENOUGH

I overheard a father and daughter at an airport in their last moments together. They had announced her plane's departure and, standing near the door, he said to his daughter, "I love you. I wish you enough."

He walked over toward the window where I was seated. Standing there, I could see he wanted and needed to cry. I tried not to intrude on his privacy, but he welcomed me in by asking, "Did you ever say goodbye to someone knowing it would be forever?"

"Yes, I have," I replied.

Recognizing that my dad's days were limited, I took the time to tell him face to face how much he meant to me. I remembered expressing my love and appreciation for all my dad had done for me. So I knew what this man was experiencing.

"Forgive me for asking, but why is this a forever goodbye?" I asked.

"I am old and she lives much too far away. I have challenges ahead and the reality is, her next trip back will be for my funeral," he said.

"When you were saying goodbye, I heard you say, 'I wish you enough.' May I ask what that meant?"

He smiled. "That's a wish that has been handed down from other generations. My parents used to say it to everyone." He paused for a moment and looked up as if trying to remember it in detail. He smiled wider. "I wish you enough sun to keep your attitude bright. I wish you enough rain to appreciate the sun more. I wish you enough happiness to keep your spirit alive. I wish you enough pain so that the smallest joys in life appear much bigger. I wish you enough gain to satisfy your wanting. I wish you enough loss to appreciate all that you possess. I wish enough 'Hellos' to get you through the final goodbye."

He began to sob and walked away.
(Original story by Bob Perks in "Chicken Soup for the Grieving Soul.")

Even a clock that is broken shows the right time twice a day.

AN INTERESTING AUDITION

Several years ago, Mount St. Vincent University in Halifax decided to start a dinner theatre in a room that was available in one of its buildings. A baritone by the name of Stephen Abbass, who was well-known in the area and an experienced performer, was approached to be a part of the new venture, and he was happy to join. Since he obviously would need a capable accompanist, the university also contacted a pianist, who happened to be me. We were to meet at the university to discuss possible programming and for our first rehearsal. Here is Abbass's account of our first meeting

"I arrived at the Mount for our first rehearsal and was introduced to my accompanist. A large used car salesman of a man, he positively bubbled over with a giddy enthusiasm which I found a trifle inappropriate considering the bar wasn't open for the occasion. I placed my sheet music on the piano in front of him and awaited my introduction...silence. To my surprise, our would-be accompanist just sat there staring at the music as if trying to decipher some ancient and mysterious code. Finally, he began stabbing at the keys. One note, a pause, his eyes searched the keyboard, then

another, and so on. This excruciating exploration of a rather simple piece continued until, finally, mercifully, shoulders drooped forward, head bowed, he admitted defeat. Trying to be helpful, I merely remarked, 'I'm waiting.'

Then he turned and without expression asked me how the piece went. I, not wishing to be rude, hummed a few bars, and he was off. His fingers embraced the keys with unrestricted joy and familiarity, and I stood in stunned silence as the old grand piano on which he played rendered up an orchestration of far greater depth and beauty than that contained in the pitiful arrangement I had brought with me. Then, as suddenly as he had begun, he stopped, and he turned and looked at me and without expression merely remarked, 'I 'm waiting.'"

As you may have figured out, I play entirely by ear.

I play by ear. What a coincidence, I listen the same way.

SMALL GESTURES SOMETIMES EQUAL BIG GAINS

Some years ago, I was part of a committee of two charged with planning an event honouring several VIPs who were to visit our city. Part of our responsibility was to choose a wine for the reception and dinner. While studying the options, I very strongly recommended a wine from the Mondavi Winery in the Napa Valley. (This was when Canadian wines were not as in vogue as they are today). My co-worker had no particular preference but wondered why I felt so strongly about using the Mondavi label. He didn't think I was a wine connoisseur, and he was right, since I drink wine only occasionally. He thought there must be a reason behind my strong preference, so I told him the following story.

A few years ago, while sharing a ride from San Francisco to Vancouver with long-time friends, the couple decided to pass through the wine country known as the Napa Valley. We visited several wineries, one of which was the Mondavi Winery. After doing the regular tour of this winery, my friends decided to explore more of the inside of the winery. It was a gorgeous day and touring the grounds looked most enjoyable, so I decided to wander outside. I came upon a flower bed of beautiful red roses that was being attended to by a lady I judged to be in her sixties. It occurred to me to give one of these roses to the lady of the couple who were so kindly giving me a lift to Vancouver. I approached the employee who was pruning the roses and asked if I might have one rose that I would give to my friend in the car. I told the lady that I hoped the Mondavis wouldn't mind my having just one rose from their beautiful assortment. As she handed me one of the roses, she smiled and said, "We certainly wouldn't mind. I am Mrs. Mondavi."

Good service is part of the image that we portray to the public. So are small gestures such as the one by Mrs. Mondavi. I will promote Mondavi Wine at every opportunity presented to me. Such is the trickle-down effect of good service and positive business gestures.

"You know that 'look' that women get when they want sex? Me neither." - Steve Martin

LEVITY

HUMOUR SNACKS!

A woman was sitting on a bench next to a homeless man. She asked him how he ended up this way.

He said, "Up until last week, I still had it all!! A cook, my clothes were washed and pressed. I had a roof over my head, I had TV, internet. I went to the gym, the pool, the library, I could still go to school.

She asked him, "What happened? Drugs? Alcohol? Divorce?"

"Oh no, nothing like that" he said. "No, I got out of prison."

John went out with some friends one night and tied one on. Knowing he was wasted, he did something that was completely new to him. He took a bus home. He arrived safe and sound, which seemed surprising as he had never driven a bus before.

Upon entering a theatre, Jim spotted a lady sitting in the lobby. She looked familiar to him so he decided to stroll over and speak to her.

"You look like Helen Brown," he said.

"You don't look so hot in blue either," she retorted.

The doctors who told Stephen Hawking he had two years to live are probably dead.

MORE HUMOROUS
SNACKS!

"Mr. Clark, I have reviewed this case very carefully," the Divorce Court Judge said, "and I've decided to give your wife $775 per month."

"That's very fair Your Honour," the husband said. "And every now and then I'll try to send her a few bucks myself."

Sign in elevator of furniture store:
Eighth floor button doesn't work. Push five and three.

A minister was completing a temperance sermon. With great emphasis, he said, "If I had all the beer in the world, I'd take it and I'd pour it into the river."

With even greater emphasis, he said, "And if I had all the wine in the world, I'd take it and pour it into the river."

And then finally, shaking his fist in the air, he said, "If I had all the whiskey in the world, I'd take it and pour into the river."

Amen.

His sermon complete, he sat down.

The song leader stood very cautiously and announced with a smile, nearly laughing, "For our closing hymn, let us sing hymn #365: *Shall We Gather at the River?*

The word "swims" upside-down is still "swims.

STILL MORE SNACKS

Some comedians never tell off-colour jokes. Here are a few of the comedians:

Shecky Greene, Red Buttons, Totie Fields, Joey Bishop, Milton Berle, Jan Murray, Danny Kaye, Henny Youngman, Buddy Hackett, Sid Caesar, Groucho Marx, Jackie Mason, Woody Allen, George Burns, Allan Sherman, Jerry Lewis, Carl Reiner, Shelley Berman, Gene Wilder, George Jessel, Alan King, Mel Brooks, Phil Silvers, Jack Carter, Rodney Dangerfield, Don Rickles, Jack Benny and many others.

Here is a sample of the kind of jokes they tell:

The doctor called Mrs. Arbuckle saying, "Mrs. Arbuckle, your cheque came back."

Mrs. Arbuckle answered, "So did my arthritis."

"I just got back from a pleasure trip. I took my mother-in-law to the airport!"

"I've been in love with the same woman for forty-nine years! If my wife ever finds out, she'll kill me."

A drunk was in front of a judge. The judge says, "You've been brought here for drinking."

The drunk says, "OK, let's get started."

The Harvard School of Medicine did a study on why ethnic women like Chinese food so much. The study revealed that this is due to Won Ton spelled backwards is Not Now.

A boy comes home from school and tells his mother he has a part in the play. She asks, "What part is it?" The boy says, "I play the part of the husband." The mother scowls and says, "Go back and tell the teacher you want a speaking part."

Two silkworms had a race. They ended up in a tie.

SNACK TIME AGAIN?

Golf Anyone?

Jim decided to tie the knot with his long-time girlfriend. One evening after the honeymoon, he was cleaning his golf shoes and his wife was watching him.

After a long period of silence, she finally said, "Honey, I've been thinking. Now that we are married, I think it's time to quit golfing. Maybe you should sell your golf clubs."

Jim looked at her in horror.

"Darling, what's wrong?" she asked.

"You sounded like my ex-wife there for a minute."

"Ex-wife!" she screamed, "I didn't know you were married before!"

"I wasn't."

For the Love of Milk

In a convent in Ireland, the ninety-nine-year-old Mother Superior lay quietly. She was dying. The nuns had gathered around her bed, laying garlands around her and trying to make her last journey comfortable. They wanted to give her warm milk to drink but she declined. One of the nuns took the glass back to the kitchen. Then, remembering a bottle of Irish whiskey that had been received as a gift the previous Christmas, she opened it and poured a generous amount into the warm milk.

Back at Mother Superior's bed, the nuns lifted her head, despite her protestations, and held the glass to her lips. The very frail nun drank a little, then a little more, and before they knew it, she had finished the whole glass down to the last drop. As her eyes brightened, the nuns thought it would be a good opportunity to have one last talk with their spiritual leader.

"Mother," the nuns asked earnestly, "please give us some of your wisdom before you leave us."

She raised herself up very slowly in the bed, looked at them and said,

"DON'T SELL THAT COW!"

When a man feels he has enough money, he wants more women. When a woman has enough money, she doesn't need a man.

FINDING A LOST CAR!

George was visiting his cousin in Toronto and decided he wanted to go shopping. So off he went to Costco, one of the largest of its kind in Canada. To get there, he borrowed his cousin's car.

After spending more than an hour in the store and spending very little money, he decided to mosey off home. Upon leaving the store and coming upon the largest parking lot he had ever seen, he realized that he didn't remember where he had parked the car. As a matter of fact, he didn't even remember what the car looked like.

An employee volunteered to help him find his car. He had a golf cart at his disposal, which would speed the task. The employee asked George what kind of car it was, as a description of it would greatly assist him in locating it. Rather embarrassed, George said he didn't know the make or the colour of the car. The only distinguishing feature about the car that he could recall was that there was a substantial dent over the right rear wheel.

With great enthusiasm, the employee set out to find the car in question. Amazingly, the car was found, dent over the right rear wheel and all. Both men stared at the car — there was a red canoe on the roof!!

Pressure is something you feel when you don't know what the hell you're doing.

GOOD SERVICE?
YES and NO

The success or failure of any enterprise depends on the talents of its people. Therefore, if machines take over the important functions of service, the chances for success are minimized. I have always been a strong advocate of good, no great, service. Most companies offer the same services and it is only the level of service that distinguishes one company from another.

For example, a company that does not answer its phones runs the risk of a lost contact with the person calling in. The first contact a customer has with a company is almost always with the person who answers the phone OR the person at the front counter.

I think it bears repeating that great service can be a company's greatest asset. Sometimes it takes a little longer to establish a company's reputation for great service, but once it is regarded as such, there is little doubt that the company will succeed. To be sure, there are other factors in play such as having a product that the public needs or knowing what you are talking about.

Many of the businesses I have been associated with depended upon great service for its success. Finance, car rentals, publishing and digital sign companies would not appear to have anything in common. My experience in these fields makes me adamant that great service is the key to success and definitely sets one company above another in whatever field it finds itself in.

The following examples of good and bad service easily illustrate why great service is so important to the success of any enterprise.

One final observation, which is excellent food for thought. If a good customer has a problem and it is handled properly, that customer becomes an even better customer as a result of any company's priority dedication to good service and facing problems head on.

While playing golf, Yogi Berra says 90% of putts that are too short don't go in.

EXQUISITE DINING

My wife and I were dining in the exquisite restaurant named SeaGlass near Sidney, BC. After placing our order, I remembered there was a business card at the cashier's desk at the front of the room, so I fetched one in case I might wish to eat there again. On my return to our table, I leaned on it slightly and forced it to tip to one side. Two full glasses of water, a cup of coffee, a Diet Coke, a glass of white wine and a small vase of fresh flowers were sent unceremoniously crashing to the floor, along with the two entrees that had just arrived.

What happened next is what real service is all about.

Three employees were instantly at the table, mopping the floor, replacing the tablecloth, cleaning up the debris on the floor and replacing the flowers. The head waitress advised us that new meals would be forthcoming as soon as possible. We were later offered a choice of several tasty desserts.

We decided to add a substantial tip to the bill when it arrived. To our surprise, there was no bill. Everything was complimentary as if the tipped table was their fault.

We have since returned to that establishment several times and recommended it to several of our friends. The excellent service we received has earned the restaurant high marks and added to their already well-deserved reputation as a great place to eat.

It took two years to build the *Titanic* and 2 hours and 40 minutes to sink it.

NOW THAT'S SERVICE!

A mature lady was coming out of a Sobeys's grocery store in Moncton with a cart full of groceries, when a driver that was going too fast and was blinded by the sun ran into her cart, knocking the lady to the ground and spreading her groceries all over the parking lot. 911 was called and she was taken to a nearby hospital. Thankfully, she was not seriously injured but did spend two nights there.

Sobeys's employees gathered up the spilled food. They notified the lady that a credit voucher for her purchases would await her on her next visit to the store. In addition, a lovely fruit basket was delivered to her in the hospital. The incident was not the responsibility of the store, but their actions certainly represented the good customer service that they preached and practised!

The government has no place in the bedrooms of the nation. - PE Trudeau

A REMARKABLE RESULT
OF GOOD SERVICE

This is a service story with a long history and a current update!

One evening several years ago, I was looking for white paint in one of the major department stores in Halifax — Eaton's or Simpson's as I recall. I went to the paint department where I was greeted by a very courteous eighteen year old. His name tag simply said "Robert." He asked me several intelligent questions about my painting mission: What kind of paint did I want? (I didn't know). On what surface will it be applied?

After this useful interrogation, Robert produced the paint I needed for my project. While paying for the paint at the customer service counter, I couldn't help being impressed by this young man. At the time, I was the owner of a Holiday Rent-Car franchise agency and was a strong advocate of excellent service. Before I left Robert that day, I asked him if he would join me for lunch some day soon. I wasn't selling anything I assured him, and he agreed to the meeting. Although, at that time there wasn't an opening in my company for a new employee, I was so taken by his professional attitude and his great knack for customer service that I hired him on the spot the day we had lunch. I truly believed that he was too good a prospect to pass up. Thus began his career in the car rental business. His aptitude for intelligent service had produced an employment opportunity!

But wait! There's much more to this story.

Robert learned our business very quickly. Along the way, he attended Dalhousie University and obtained his degree in business administration all the while maintaining an ongoing work relationship with Holiday. Eventually he became a part owner and remained as such until I sold the company to Avis several years later.

Today, after some forty years in the industry, Robert is still with Avis but as general manager of the new Avis/Budget organization. He is responsible for operations for all of the Maritime Provinces. This includes thirty-five rental outlets and 6,000 vehicles. The good service he provided 40 years ago paid off handsomely and provided a very meaningful and satisfying career for him.

It takes thousands of nuts to construct an automobile, but only one nut to scatter them all over the road.

MacArthur's House Flower & Gift Shop

10%

GREAT FLOWER SERVICE ACROSS THE COUNTRY

I had a sister who lived in Moncton, NB, before she recently passed away. Three years ago, I wanted to acknowledge her July birthday and decided to send her some flowers. I went on the internet and brought up flower shops in Moncton. There were several listed there of course, but the ad that caught my eye was the one from McArthur's Flowers, a shop that I was familiar with, having lived in Moncton years ago. I was delighted to be reminded of their operation. Their ad was by far the best on that site. I phoned them and placed an order for a dozen roses to be delivered to my sister. They arrived promptly and the product they sent was more than satisfactory and pleased my sister to no end.

But that isn't the best part of the service story.

The following year, late in June, I received a phone call from that same flower shop (keep in mind that I live in Victoria, BC, and they are in Moncton, NB). The florist asked if I wanted to send flowers to my sister as I had the previous year. To top it off, they offered a 10% discount. *What a great follow-up system they have in place*, I thought. Totally impressed, this time I ordered a potted plant which, as in the previous year, was delivered promptly and received appreciative accolades from my sister.

A great example of great service in action.

A sign in a shoe repair store:
    We will heel you,
        We will save your sole,
            We will even dye for you.

GOING THE EXTRA MILE

As the event coordinator for a convention, I went to a print shop named Bayside Print and ordered brochures for one of the meetings to be held later in the week. A few days later, I dropped in to the printer to pick up the brochures. To my horror, I discovered that they had not been folded. I needed the brochures that evening and the printer was about to close.

An accommodating employee insisted on staying and putting the brochures through the folding machine. He did it willingly and cheerfully. He finished at 5:30 and was still smiling. (No, he was not one of the owners.) Bayside Print received all my future printing business, which, as it turned out, was considerable.

Which letter is silent in the word "Scent," the S or the C?

EXPENSIVE BUT THE RIGHT THING

Some years ago when I was a publisher in Halifax, I was fortunate enough to get the rights to publish the visitor guide for the cities of Halifax and Dartmouth. (All the cities in the area have since amalgamated but back then, the tourism departments of the two main cities were operated separately). My company, Metro Guide Publishing, gathered tourist information and maps from the two cities and combined them in one guide, which would then be distributed free of charge through the tourist associations of the two cities. To cover the cost of producing what turned out to be an excellent publication, ads were sold in both cities resulting in a product that had a circulation of 225,000 copies.

While preparing the final stages of the publication, I was advised that an ad, which had been committed by a fairly large local hotel chain, had not yet arrived. We were not successful in reaching the person who had placed the ad, and we were about to go to press. We had a substantial amount of information about this hotel chain on hand, so I decided we should create an ad ourselves and proceed with the printing of the guide. Our designer was in the process of completing another ad and, horror of horrors, used the wrong number in the ad that we were producing for the hotel group. To make matters worse, the number we used in the hotel chain ad was one of the chain's competitors (albeit a small one)!

When the publication reached the public, I received an urgent phone call from the owner of the hotel chain. He requested — no, ordered — my presence in his office to protest the error we had made in his ad. He was, of course, correct but his well-known reputation for being cantankerous was very much in evidence as I sat in his office and listened to his unrelenting verbiage. I distinctly remember his saying, "This will cost you millions, Mr. LeBlanc, millions."

I told him to leave it with me and I would address the problem.

I did two things. First, I contacted the much smaller competitor hotel who agreed to forward on any inquiries that they received that were obviously for the larger chain. Then, after further investigation, I learned that only about 8,000 of the 225,000 copies we had printed were actually in circulation. The undistributed copies were being held in a warehouse being used by Tourism Halifax. I hired eight eight students who, using stickers that I provided, changed the phone number in all of the remaining copies. It took a lot of time and money to accomplish this, but it was our error and had to be done. Our reputation for excellent service and for reliability was, after all, at stake.

This satisfied the owner of the hotel chain, not that he ever thanked us for our efforts. The upside of all this is that the word got around the cities of the measures we had taken to correct our error. We received nothing but praise from other members of the tourism industry for our excellent recovery. Many sympathized that we had to deal with a particularly difficult situation and owner.

Make a friend when you don't need one.

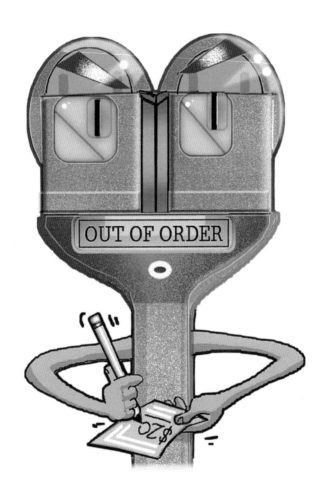

BAD SERVICE BITES

Parking meters are a bane to some drivers, but the reality is they keep cars moving along. Drivers who work in the area cannot park all day and meter are a source of income for the city.

I was looking for a parking meter spot when I saw an empty space. I manoeuvred my car into the spot and plugged the meter when I noticed it was out of order. Just then, a commissionaire happened by and I pointed out the situation to him. He told me that if I parked there, he would give me a ticket even though the meter was inoperative. Awful service by a city employee.

Hydro companies are traditionally much like large civil service offices where getting an answer to a question or speaking to a real person is an ordeal.

A friend whose mother had moved was attempting to clean up some loose ends at Mom's former residence. She phoned the hydro people and was kept on the line for an inordinate length of time before finally speaking to a real person. (The phone machine's runaround was pathetic to say the least.) She was

calling to cancel the service at her mom's condo and was told they needed a copy of the power of attorney in order to comply. Faxing the document would suffice. After completing this request, she phoned back and suffered the same fate as the first call — a very long wait. Finally, the person came on the phone and guess what? She advised my friend that the service had been cancelled the previous week by her mother (who had, of course, neglected to tell her daughter).

Why could the employee not have passed on that information on the first call? Unbelievable!

There is an area on the waterfront in Halifax, Nova Scotia, called Historic Properties. It has several restaurants, boutiques and gift shops that specialize in typical Maritime food, souvenirs and other merchandise. While planning a trip out west, I ventured into one of the gift shops for the purpose of buying three items to give to friends I would be visiting on my trip. There were several items that would do the trick, but there was only one clerk in the shop busy talking on the phone (to her boyfriend it sounded like). Though I tried to get her attention, she continued to ignore me and continued her phone conversation.

I have been a strong advocate of good service all my business life and finding none in this establishment, I left. Two doors down, I found another shop of the same type and promptly bought over $100 worth of goods to take with me on my trip. I am sure the clerk in the first shop told the owner that business was slow that morning. He obviously had not spent any time, money or effort to properly train the young clerk in the art of good customer service.

It's not premarital sex if you have no intention of getting married.

BOTTOMLESS???

When having lunch one day at a well-known, well-respected restaurant in Victoria, BC, I ordered my usual Diet Coke. Eventually, I asked the waiter if the drink was "bottomless" — restaurant parlance for free refills. The cost of the original drink was $2.95, and I was told a refill would be an additional $1.50. The cost of a refill to the restaurant is approximately .10!!! (or a little more). I spoke to the lady in charge and she reinforced the policy! I suggested she call three or four of their competitors and ascertain her competition's policies.

On my next and last visit to this restaurant, I again spoke to the same lady in charge. She stated she had addressed the "refill" situation and management held firm on their policy.

I have inquired at several other restaurants in the area and NONE of them charge for refills. In fact, in many instances, the waiter, seeing the drink nearing the bottom of the glass, asks if the patron would like a refill! Now that's service!

The small amount of profit derived from the $1.50 refill cost will in no way offset the negative aspect of this policy. Customers are aware of such policies and often have negative vibes towards that particular restaurant.

An update on the above story: the restaurant now practices "bottomless."

Apple founder, Steve Jobs, didn't let his kids use iPads.

EXCUSES, EXCUSES, EXCUSES

A few years ago, I was in need of a CD of the cast of *Showboat* for a production I was putting together. I dropped into Sam the Record Man in downtown Halifax to purchase one but unfortunately it was not in stock. I was advised they could order one for me that would arrive in a week or less. I said OK since it suited my purpose at the time. I left my business card to facilitate contact.

Three weeks later when I needed the CD, I went to the store to inquire about my order. The clerk went to the back of the store and returned with the disc, which had my business card Scotch-taped to it.

"Oh, the disc has been here for a couple of weeks," the clerk said, "and we have been unable to reach you."

I found that strange since, in my business, we are adamant about staff answering the phone when we are open, which is 9 to 5 each day. An answering machine takes calls when we are closed. I was then informed that "call back" calls are done in the evening when the store isn't busy. No explanation was given as to why no message was left on my machine to inform me that the disc was in.

Good service is about going the extra mile to solve a problem, not just coming up with some excuse as to why a certain thing wasn't done. By the way, that store is now out of business!!

At an electric company: we would be delighted if you send in your payment.
If you don't, you will be.

NO HST

In Halifax, a newly married couple wished to buy a new microwave and a coffee table. An ad in the local newspaper advertised a "no GST sale" at a major department store between 8 a.m. and 10 a.m. on Saturday. This piqued their interest and they arrived at the store around 9 a.m. After a lengthy discussion with a sales representative, they decided to think about the microwave purchase and proceeded to another section of the store where they ordered a coffee table. They also discussed the microwave and decided they would buy it.

Upon returning to the first department, they located the salesperson that had spent close to a half hour with them earlier in the morning. They indicated their desire to purchase the microwave but the salesperson advised them that the "no GST sale" ended at 10 a.m. and since it was now 10:05 a.m., they would not qualify for the sale discount! The couple bought a microwave elsewhere and also cancelled the order for the coffee table.

The salesperson was at fault for not honoring the "no GST" deal for these people. He was not the only one at fault in this situation. Had the salesperson been properly trained and encouraged to use good judgment when needed, and been confident of support from superiors, this situation would not have materialized.

Do twins ever realize that one of them is unplanned?

EMPLOYEES WHO NEED A PERMANENT VACATION

At 9 a.m. one morning, I phoned the office of John Stratton, an executive friend, who's valuable counsel I sought for a project I was working on. I was advised that he wasn't in the office. Would I like to leave a callback number? I did and I did.

At around 3 p.m. the same day, I realized I had not heard from him and tried his office again. I was told by the same receptionist that he was not in and would I like to leave a message for him. I told her that I had called earlier in the day and had not heard from him.

"Is he expected in soon?" I inquired.

"Mr. Stratton left for a three-week vacation yesterday," she said.

Why in heaven's name would she not provide that information when I called the first time? The very first contact the public has with a company is very likely on the phone. The importance of the person answering the phone cannot possibly be overstated.

A company that does not give answering the phone high priority is operating ineffectively.

If you ever get lost in the woods, just start talking politics and someone will show up to argue with you.

LETTER TO A NEW YORK BANK

This is a letter sent to a NYC bank by a customer. The manager of the bank forwarded it to a *New York* newspaper hoping they would print it. They did!

Dear Sir:

I am writing to thank you for bouncing my cheque with which I endeavoured to pay my plumber last month. By my calculations, three nanoseconds must have elapsed between his presenting the cheque and the arrival in my account of the funds needed to honor it. I refer, of course, to the automatic monthly deposit of my entire salary, an arrangement which, I admit, has been in place for only eight years. You are to be commended for seizing that brief window of opportunity, and also for debiting my account $50 by way of penalty for the inconvenience caused to your bank. My thankfulness springs from the manner in which this incident *has caused me to rethink my errant financial ways.*

I noticed that whereas I personally attend to your telephone calls and letters, when I try to contact you, I am confronted by the impersonal, overcharging, pre-recorded faceless entity which your bank has become. From now on, I, like you, choose only to deal with a flesh-and-blood person. My mortgage and loan repayments will, therefore and hereafter, no longer be automatic, but will arrive at your bank, by cheque, addressed personally, and confidentially, to an employee at your bank whom you must nominate. Be aware that it is an offence under the Postal Act for any other person to open such an envelope. Please find attached an Application Contact Status which I require your chosen employee to complete. I am sorry it runs to eight pages, but in order that I know as much about him or her as your bank knows about me, there is no alternative.

Please note that all copies of his or her medical history must be countersigned by a Notary Public, and the mandatory details of his/her financial situation income, debts, assets and liabilities must be accompanied by documented proof. In due course, I will issue your employee with a PIN number which he/she must quote in dealings with me. I regret that it cannot be shorter than 28 digits but, again, I have modelled it on the number of button presses required to access my account balance on your phone bank service. As they say, imitation is the sincerest form of flattery.

Let me level the playing field even further. Press buttons as follow:

1 - To make an appointment to see me.

2 - To query a missing payment.

3 - To transfer the call to my living room in case I am there.

4 - To transfer the call to my bedroom in case I am sleeping.

5 - To transfer the call to my toilet in case I am attending to nature.

6 - To transfer the call to my mobile phone if I am not at home.

7 - To leave a message on my computer, a password to access my computer is required. A password will be communicated at a later date to the authorized contact.

8 - To return to the main menu and to listen to options 1 through 7.

9 - To make a general complaint or inquiry. The contact will then be put on hold, pending the attention of my automated answering service. While this may, on occasion, involve a lengthy wait, uplifting music will play for the duration of the call.

Regrettably, but again following your example, I must also levy an establishment fee to cover the setting up of this new arrangement. May I wish you a happy, if ever-so-slightly less prosperous day.

Your humble client.

Age is a matter of mind over matter. If you don't mind, it doesn't matter. - Satchel Paige

A BANK ADVENTURE

Several years ago, I wished to speak to an individual in the Royal Bank branch that I do business with in Halifax. I looked up the number for the branch in the phone directory and dialed. A gentleman answered and I explained that I wished to speak to a lady in that branch. However, I could not recall this lady's name but proceeded to describe the lady in question saying that she had a cast on her foot.

The gentleman said he was sorry, but he did not know this person. I said, "How many people in your branch have a cast on their foot? Surely that is enough to describe the person I wish to speak to." Only then did he advise me that he was speaking to me from Calgary. Keep in mind that the number I dialed was listed in the phone directory as a local number! A cost-saving measure no doubt, but it took some time before I finally got through to the branch itself.

The next year, I again attempted to reach a different Royal Bank branch. I again phoned the number in the directory. This time I got recordings — the usual: for this kind of information, push one, etc., etc. I was also asked to punch in my client card number. Another recording informed me that due to the high volume of calls there would be a delay in answering my call — would I like to phone again later? (Certainly not!) Occasionally, a recorded voice would come on selling the virtues of Royal's services such as Visa and online banking.

Finally, I got a real person. Since I was in the throes of preparing this book and had less than satisfactory telephone experiences in the past, I had decided to use my stopwatch to monitor the amount of time it took to reach the person I was calling. Are you ready for it? Seven minutes and twenty-six seconds!!

Major banks spend millions of dollars on advertising to encourage us to use their services. Yet, they do not practice good customer service by answering their phones except by machine. Go figure.

I'm an excellent housekeeper. Every time I get a divorce, I keep the house. - Zsa Zsa Gabor

MEETING ARNOLD PALMER

There are many superheroes in the world of sport. Those who have surpassed their contemporaries with feats above and beyond the norm. People such as Babe Ruth, Michael Jordan, Vince Lombardi and Billy Jean King come to mind.

But none have had the impact on their sport in terms of growth and acceptance by the public than Arnold Palmer. His accomplishments on and off the field are legend and will probably never be matched.

While living in Montreal, I had the opportunity to attend the Canadian Open which was being held in the area at the time. I followed Palmer for one of his rounds. He parred every hole from one to seventeen and then sank a long snaky putt for a birdie on his last hole.

As he walked off the eighteenth green, I approached him and told him I would appreciate shaking his hand. He did so willingly and was very courteous to say the least. A true legend, of that there is no doubt, and he comported himself in a very human and ordinary way. This is a characteristic I believe is common in all great athletes.

Palmer literally transformed professional golf from anonymity to the great sport it has become today. The huge amounts of money that today's golfers earn can be attributed to Palmer's influence on the game. He captured the imagination of the golfing public and made watching golf on T.V. a new and exciting pastime. For the record, he was also the driving force behind what we know today as the Golf Channel.

If you rip a hole in a net, there are fewer holes in it than there were before.

MORE STORIES

TV TIDBITS

Many of us who enjoy watching TV, especially the late-night talk shows, have often commented on the length of commercials that sometimes seem endless. To be sure, TV entertainment depends on the money received from running commercials, and thanks to the commercials, we are royally entertained. But, the length of them can be frustrating at times.

Just to make a point, I timed the length of commercials and was not particularly surprised by the results — they confirmed my thoughts. In fact, my timing revealed the average length of a commercial break is three minutes. HOWEVER, there are often times when a break will last as long as eight minutes with a short break in the middle that makes it seem like the commercial is over, but it is not.

Another observation about TV commercials is that, probably to prevent channel surfing, stations break for commercials at exactly the same time, sports events excluded, although they quite frequently coincided.

It is also interesting to note that TV stations are traditionally unbiased in their reporting — indeed, that should be the norm. But it is obvious that CNN favors the Democrats and is decidedly anti-Trump, whereas Fox News is unabashedly pro-Trump.

Tomorrow belongs to those who see it coming.

AUTO OBSERVATIONS

Several years ago, automobile dealers handled new models in a much different way than they do today. For example, manufacturers introduced their new models in the fall. They kept the public in the dark — even covering up models that had already arrived — in order to be able to have a big surprise showing of the new models when "Showtime" was at hand. Back then, cars had their own distinct style whereas today, many models resemble each other to the point that it is not easy to distinguish one model from another.

Before the advent of foreign-made vehicles, most cars were made either made by Ford, General Motors or Chrysler. Also, if an individual was fortunate enough to have a franchise from one of these major manufacturers, he was definitely not allowed to have more than one franchise (i.e., a Ford dealer was not allowed to purchase a Chrysler franchise — it just was not permitted by the manufacturers).

This is no longer the case. Today, as an example, the Jim Pattison Group has Vancouver, BC, as its headquarters. Their portfolio includes such makes as Toyota, Volvo, Subaru, Lexus, Hyundai, Audi, Volkswagen and Chrysler.

Times have changed! It was always an exciting time of the year trying to guess which automobile manufacturer had created the most interesting and memorable new styled car.

The biggest waste of manpower is to want to change something that's not changeable!

A SENIOR'S EXERCISE?

1. Begin by standing on a comfortable surface where you have plenty of room on each side.

2. With a 5lb potato bag in each hand, extend your arms straight out from your sides and hold them as long as you can. Try to reach a full minute, and then relax.

3. Each day you'll find that you can hold this position for just a bit longer. After a couple of weeks, move up to 10lb potato bags.

4. Then try 50lb potato bags and then eventually try to get to where you can lift a 100lb potato bag in each hand and hold your arms straight for more than a full minute.

5. After you feel confident at that level, put a potato in each bag.

What did the left eye say to the right eye? Between us, something smells.

HIGH BEAMS
AND SIRENS

I was a twenty-two-year-old finance company trainee who lived and worked in a small Nova Scotia town. While living there, I arranged for room and board with the Langille family. Mr. Langille was in sales and was also the fire chief of the local volunteer fire department.

I felt extremely lucky to be living with the Langilles. The meals were exceptional and I was treated like a member of the family (which consisted of two other children).

One evening as I was preparing to go to the movies, Mr. Langille offered me the use of his car. After the movie, which ended early, I took my friend for a drive down the river. As I was returning to town, the ongoing traffic necessitated my lowering the high beams. Immediately, there was the loud sound of a siren, louder than I had ever heard before. Thinking there was an ambulance, police car or fire truck behind me, I, of course, pulled over. I quickly realized what had occurred. The vintage of the car I was driving did not have a lever on the steering wheel to lower high beams. Instead, there was a button on the floor for that purpose. It is located right beside the dimmer, and when pressed, triggers the siren that I heard. Mr. Langille had it installed for use when performing his duties as the local fire chief. I had accidentally activated the siren when attempting to dim the lights!

To say that I was frightened would be putting it mildly. Mr. Langille and I shared a good laugh about it later. It didn't seem funny at the time!

Silence is often misinterpreted but never misquoted.

MYTHS ABOUT RUNNING A SMALL BUSINESS

1. Work on your business, not in it!
   - Important to do both.

2. Fast growth is mandatory and good!
   - Bad debt is corrosive to growth — it eats at cash flow.

3. Every job must be filled!
   - Make sure hiring is absolutely necessary before taking that leap.

4. You need to pay the big bucks!
   - Perks are more important than money.

5. Small businesses need to think small!
   - Dare to dream and think big!

6. Small businesses are more flexible!
   - Not when it comes to cash flow.

7. You're all alone in it!
   - Advisory groups are available and desirable.

8. You can't afford to market!
  - Never before has it been so simple to market you own business.

The above is a short excerpt of an article written by Kerry Slavens that appeared in the Oct/Nov 2019 issue of Douglas Magazine. *An award winning magazine,* Douglas *is one of (if not "the") finest business magazines now circulating in the Victoria, BC, market. Its circulation of 30,000 per issue reaches the business community as well as an important segment of the Victoria residential community.*

Nobody ever goes there, it's always full. - Yogi Berra

RODGERS & HAMMERSTEIN

Can you guess who wrote the lyrics to the song *When I Grow Too Old to Dream?* The answer will surprise you. It was none other than Oscar Hammerstein 11. Sigmund Romberg wrote the music and Hammerstein provided the lyrics. The year was 1934.

Some of the facts about the life of Hammerstein:

He was born in 1895 and died in 1960.

His claim to fame was his outstanding work as a lyricist of popular and Broadway music.

He is best known for his collaboration with Richard Rodgers, but his musical career started long before that well-known association.

His first major partnership was with Sigmund Romberg (who was best known for *The Student Prince*). This relationship lasted several years after which Hammerstein partnered with the prolific composer, Jerome Kern.

With Kern, Hammerstein penned the lyrics for the Broadway classic *Showboat*. Well-known ballads by this team include *Who*, *The Song is You* and the immortal *All the Things You Are*. During World War II, he and Kern produced a tribute to the city of Paris, a ballad called *The Last Time I Saw Paris*.

Eventually, Hammerstein's partnership with Jerome Kern ended. At that time, Rodgers was in partnership with lyricist Lorenz Hart. This talented duo was responsible for such hits as *Lover*, *Small Hotel*, *Manhattan*, *Bewitched*, *Blue Moon*, *With a Song in My Heart* and *My Funny Valentine*. They collaborated on several movies and composed the scores for twenty-six Broadway productions. Hart had a problem with alcohol and eventually succumbed to the disease.

When a planned Broadway adaptation of the book *Green Grow the Lilacs* required new composers, Rodgers and Hammerstein were pressed into service. Their premiere show was *Oklahoma!* — the first of several hits this talented duo penned. Among others, they were responsible for such shows as *The Sound of Music, Flower Drum Song*, *South Pacific*, *Carousel* and *The King and I*. Also in their vast repertoire is the music for the movie version of *Cinderella* in 1957.

Rodgers died in 1979 at the age of 77.

Rodgers & Hammerstein II are definitely one of the great legends of the Broadway stage's renowned history. Their music will live forever in the hearts of all fans of the musical genre.

I'd rather see two men holding hands than two men holding guns!

THE CBC'S HOCKEY KNOWLEDGE

Consider this totally FICTITIOUS scenario:

What if Peter Mansbridge, in his anchor position at the CBC, had become a highly-regarded spokesman for the election campaign of former prime minister, Stephen Harper? What if he championed Harper on every newscast and was a 100% supporter of all of Harper's policies and programs? Imagine if he used his unique position at CBC to praise Harper at every opportunity, all the while being extremely critical of Trudeau and Mulcair, Harper's opponents. What if Mansbridge also reminisced about past Conservative icons, helping to bring fame to these long-gone politicians?

Would the CBC tolerate such a situation? Their treatment of Evan Solomon and Jian Ghomeshi indicates it wouldn't accept any scenario that would tarnish the golden reputation and credibility of the CBC.

OK, so consider this ACTUAL scenario:

One of the CBC's highest rated and presumably very profitable programs is the legendary Saturday night *Hockey Night in Canada*. One of the segments of this show is called *Coach's Corner with Don Cherry*. If Mansbridge, as pictured in our fictitious scenario, would incur the wrath of the CBC if he blatantly supported Stephen Harper, why does the network tolerate one of its commentators openly supporting the Toronto Maple Leafs and the Boston Bruins with no attempt whatever at being non-partisan?

The 2016 "Winter Classic" featured the Montreal Canadiens and the Boston Bruins in a highly-publicized outdoor NHL game, and it was broadcast by *Hockey Night in Canada*. Cherry wore Boston Bruins garb while standing with the hierarchy of the Boston Bruins, including legendary defenceman Bobby Orr. Cherry had not coached nor had Orr played in the NHL since the '70s. That is many years ago, yet Cherry continued to rave on about Orr. To be sure, he was an outstanding player, but Cherry's reminiscing about him during several telecasts is not in keeping with the high standards that the CBC expects from all of its other commentators.

Why the double standard here, CBC? Is this in keeping with your mandate? Quite an inconsistency!

Editor's note: Cherry has since been replaced due to his comments on immigrants.

A bad rower blames the oar.

PUNS

WIRE A RESERVATION

An indigenous chief of a tribe, not wanting his eldest son, Andrew, to be uneducated and live his life on the reservation, sent Andrew to university where he received his diploma in electrical engineering. Since the whole reservation had contributed to the cost of his education, he decided to do something for the tribe as a thank you for their assistance.

The entrance of the reservation had a large structure to which Andrew affixed a large stuffed moose head. He then took advantage of his training and installed lights in each of the eyes. As a result, when daylight was gone, the lighted moose head could be seen from great distances.

It was said that he was the first to wire a head for a reservation.

Nearly all men can stand adversity,
but if you want to test a man's character, give him power. - Abraham Lincoln

PUNNY LINES

I wondered why the baseball kept getting bigger. Then it hit me!

Sign on a blinds and curtains truck: "Blind Man Driving."

Sign on a plumber's truck: "Don't sleep with a drip. Call your plumber."

Sign on an optometrist's office: "If you can't see what you're looking for, you're in the right place."

Sign on a tire shop: "Invite us to your next blowout."

Sign on an electrician's truck: "Let us remove your shorts."

Sign at a car dealership: "The best way to get back on your feet is to miss a car payment."

Sign at a radiator shop: "Best place in town to take a leak."

Sign at a funeral home: "Drive carefully, we'll wait."

A man who is addicted to drinking brake fluid says he can stop anytime.

When the fog lifts in Los Angeles, UCLA.

"I have a split personality," says Tom being frank.

A thief who stole a calendar got twelve months.

With her marriage, she got a new name and a dress.

To write with a broken pencil is pointless.

What's the difference between a hippo and a Zippo? One is heavy and the other is a little lighter.

I lost my job at the bank on my first day. A lady asked me to check her balance so I pushed her.

I stayed up all night to see where the sun went, and then it dawned on me.

Acupuncture is a jab well done.

I have a few jokes about unemployed people, but none of them work.

What do you call an arrogant criminal going down the stairs? A condescending con descending.

A man walked into the doctor's office and said, "Doctor, I can't stop singing the *Green, Green Grass of Home*."

The doctor said, "That sounds like Tom Jones syndrome to me."

"Is it common?" he asked.

"*It's Not Unusual*."

Nationalism is cured by travelling.

A REAL GROANER

I was brought up in Moncton, New Brunswick, in a French Acadian home that featured Acadian food, great hospitality and lots of music. We truly had a very musical home. In fact, it was so musical that even the sewing machine was a Singer!

A grenade thrown into a kitchen in France would result in Linoleum Blownapart.

HOW TO CALL
THE POLICE

George was on his way to bed one night when he noticed activity in his shed at the back of the house. There were people in his shed stealing things.

He phoned the police who asked if there was someone in his house. He replied no but there were some people in his garden shed and they appeared to be stealing things.

The dispatcher said that all patrols were busy. "Lock your doors and one of our officers will be along as soon as one is available."

George said OK, but after waiting no more than a minute, he called the police again. He said, "I just phoned you a few minutes ago to report that someone was burglarizing my shed. You don't have to worry about these burglars anymore. I just shot them, and I think they're both dead."

Within five minutes, several police cars, a SWAT team, a fire truck and an ambulance arrived and caught the burglars red-handed.

One of the policemen asked George, "I thought you said you shot them," to which

George replied, "I thought you said that everyone was busy."

Do you know just how much seniors appreciate a phone call? They didn't abandon you when you were small, so don't abandon them now.

TIME WAITS FOR NO ONE

To realize the value of ten years, ask a newly divorced couple.

To realize the value of one year, ask a student who has failed a final exam.

To realize the value of nine months, ask a woman who gave birth to a still-born.

To realize the value of one month, ask a mother who has given birth to a premature baby.

To realize the value of one week, ask the editor of a weekly newspaper.

To realize the value of one hour, ask the lovers who are waiting to meet.

TO REALIZE THE VALUE OF ONE MINUTE, ASK THE PERSON WHO HAS MISSED THE BUS, TRAIN OR PLANE.

To realize the value of one second, ask a person who has survived an accident.

To realize the value of one millisecond, ask the person who won a silver medal in the Olympics.

Time waits for no one. Treasure every moment you have. You will treasure it even more when you can share it with someone special.

Author unknown

Life is a journey, not a destination.

THE JACKET

Someone said to me the other day, "My that's a really nice jacket." *If you only knew*, I thought. Then yesterday, I received the same compliment about my jacket. Again, I thought about the story behind "the jacket," so perhaps it's time I explain its origin.

I was on a return trip, by car, from New York heading for home in Halifax. Upon passing a factory outlet store in Maine, I decided to stop and look around. I didn't think I really needed anything, but I wanted a break from driving and this outlet store was just what the doctor ordered.

While browsing around the store, I spotted a display of jackets that were greatly reduced in price. I fancied a suede jacket that was on sale and decided to try it on. I loved it instantly. The only problem was that it didn't fit me properly. The sleeves were much too short. It was a great colour (light brown beige), the price was very enticing, it had a black lining and, except for the length of the sleeves, was perfect! It was the only one left of its ilk in the store. Oh my, what to do??

Well, short sleeves and all, I bought it anyway and have happily worn it ever since.

What makes this story interesting is that the above narrative took place in 1992! So, the jacket is thirty-four years old. Obviously, it still looks good and compliments in its regard are always surprising but nonetheless appreciated. In today's styles, the short sleeves are right up to date. The cuffs are navy blue wool and, when wearing a long-sleeved navy shirt underneath it, there is a perfect colour blend even though the sleeves are too short.

I'm glad that those who have noticed the jacket appreciate it as much as I do!

Even a fish wouldn't get in trouble if it kept its mouth shut.

MOOSEHEAD IN NEW ORLEANS

New Orleans is an interesting city, most particularly to anyone who is interested in jazz and excellent cuisine. One has only to walk down Bourbon Street to prove this point. Doors to the individual establishments are always open, and the sound of jazz emanates from each of them, creating a party atmosphere not found anywhere else in North America. The restaurants in this area are second to none. The city is also known for its incredible annual Mardi Gras celebration.

It has a population of 391,006 as of the 2018 census. It is often referred to a "The Big Easy." It has a melange of French, African and American cultures and is one of the top destinations for tourism in the world.

I was recently in this wonderful city to finalize arrangements for an upcoming convention of some 200 attendees. Upon visiting a club that was owned by none other than the great Al Hirt, I was able to arrange for our group to take over his whole club for the evening. He was a most gracious host and a great time was had by all.

To finalize the arrangements for this wonderful evening, I met Mr. Hirt in his private office at the rear of the club. And what to my wondering eyes did I spy on the top of his desk, but a can of Moosehead beer. Of course, there is nothing wrong with having a beer in one's own office but the most interesting observation made by Mr. Hirt was that Moosehead is the only beer he could/would drink. He had it shipped in, by the case, from Saint John, NB, where it is produced!!

Aside from the Acadian connection, obviously New Orleans and Saint John, NB, have Moosehead beer in common.

Beer is made by man, wine by God.

MAJOR LEAGUE COINCIDENCES

We have all had some interesting coincidences in our lives. Here are a few of mine.

I was living in Moncton and planning a trip to New York City for the purpose of seeing some Major League Baseball games. (This was before the advent of the Expos in Montreal.) I mentioned my trip to a friend and he reminded me that a mutual friend of ours, lets call him Jake, was now living in New York. I told him that since Jake lived on Long Island, it was doubtful I would see him on this trip.

While in New York, I visited Shea Stadium, home of the New York Mets. Keep in mind that this stadium holds around 55,000 fans and has over thirty entrances. It was a sell-out that day. While leaving the stadium after the game, I noticed someone walking ahead of me who looked familiar. Sure enough, it was Jake!! Quite a coincidence wasn't it?

If you must throw cold water on everything, then get a job as a fireman.

UNBELIEVABLE BORDER CROSSING

When motoring from San Francisco to Vancouver, I obviously had to pass through customs at the Canadian border. When I arrived at the customs area there were no less than twelve lanes that I could enter. I chose a lane, and since I had items to declare, I was pointed to a nearby building to fill out the proper forms. Once inside, there were at least a dozen more positions for me to choose from and do my business. When I came to an agent, I handed my passport and other relative information to the lady in the booth. She looked at my name and asked where I lived. I told her Halifax, Nova Scotia. The agent casually asked if I knew such and such a street. I asked the reason for her inquiry and she said that a young man from that street was coming to visit her the very next week. The street she asked about was the street on which my brother lives, and the young man is my nephew. Considering the number of gates I could have chosen entering the compound as well as the numerous positions of agents inside the building, the odds of my connecting with this particular agent would be very low. Amazing!!

Why was 6 afraid of 7. Because 7, 8, 9.

A COINCIDENCE IN THE BEDROOM

Several years ago, I travelled to our branch in Calgary as part of my duties as vice president of operations for Holiday Rent a Car. Although I was working out of London, Ontario, the owners in Calgary knew I was originally from Halifax. As we were on our way out to lunch, they mentioned that there were a couple of young men who were operating a business nearby that they knew were from Halifax. As luck would have it, they were standing outside their business as we drove by on our way to lunch, so we stopped. I asked lots of questions such as who the parents were etc., but nothing rang a bell. When I asked one of them which street he lived on when in Halifax, he said I probably would not be familiar with it. Just to keep the conversation going, I asked him the name of the street. It was West Street, an area I had lived in for about a year. Further discussions revealed that his home had been sold to the folks I was boarding with at the time, and we had actually slept in the same bedroom!!!!

Imagine that!!!

A camel is a horse designed by a committee.

SURPRISING
MEDICAL REPORT

Raymond: Well if it isn't my good friend, Sammy. How have you been? Haven't seen you for several years. I can't believe we haven't kept in touch. I was glad to hear you were back in town. Hope you are here to stay. So tell me, I'll ask again, how have you been? You look just great.

Sammy: Well, I am feeling just fine thank you. And look at you, how old are you now, 23? 24?

Raymond: I am now, believe it or not, 27. How about you?

Sammy: I will be 85 in two weeks. I certainly have been through a few health situations over the years. I'm finding it happens as you get older.

Raymond: Oh! What are they??

Sammy: There have been many health problems, but I'm sure you don't want to hear all of that.

Raymond: Absolutely, I want to hear all of it.

Sammy: Very well, here goes. My eyesight was giving me problems, so I had two cataract operations and my eyesight is much better now although I still need to wear eyeglasses for reading. My mood swings were totally unpredictable, bordering on depression. My doctor prescribed Wellbutrin, which he says I will need to take for the rest of my life. I must admit though, that these pills really do the job. Depression never rears its head, not anymore.

Several years ago, I had a hip replacement.

I have something called atrial fibrillation. My heartbeat is irregular and needs to be regulated by medication. This is quite serious and unpredictable but so far, all is well. I am obliged to take Warfarin. The doses need to be regulated so I have blood tests every three weeks.

My energy levels are suspect due to a deficiency of B-12 in my system. As a result, I have B-12 injections once monthly to make up for this.

Like many men my age, my prostate showed the presence of cancer. My PSA reading was around 14 and should be more like 4 or 5. After thirty-five short cancer treatments via radiation, my prostate reading was reduced to .8 and is no longer a problem!

I have diabetes 2. As a result, my doctor has prescribed Crestor and I do blood tests about once a week to check my blood sugar level. It is currently at 6.0, which I understand is more than satisfactory.

I think that covers everything I've been dealing with these past several years. What about you? Tell me all about what's been happening in your life.

Raymond: (His eyes bulged out and he looked thoughtful). The only thing I can think of is that I have a plantar wart on the bottom of one foot but the doctor is treating it. Listening to all your aches and pains, old age is not something I am really looking forward to.

At the end of the day people won't remember what you said or did but will remember how you made them feel. - Maya Angelou

COUNTING SHEEP

There is an adage, or even an unproven historical tale, that counting sheep helps one to go to sleep at night. In my opinion, there is a much better way to accomplish the same thing. Instead of counting sheep, I have found that recalling famous people is more effective. There are two ways to actually do this. The first is to think about, not necessarily count, well-known celebrities in any field that you have actually met or spoken to. To illustrate, here is a personal list of such people I have encountered.

Cleo Laine, John Dankworth, Mitch Miller, Roger Williams, Arnold Palmer, Arthur Fiedler, Rebecca Luker, Rocket Richard, Jean Beliveau, Guy Lafleur, Victor Garber, Lucy Simon, Howard Cable, Don Herron, Michael Spinks, Greg Proop, Ian Tyson, Spiro Malas, John Arpin, George Feyer, Rita MacNeil, Anne Murray, the Royal Canadian Air Farce, Jackie Mason, Al Hirt, Pete Fountain, Buddy Hackett, Frank McKenna, Jodi Benson, Lorie Kane.

Use a slightly different method by thinking about famous people you have encountered, but not actually met or spoken to. Here is my list of such people.

André Gagnon, Sean Hayes, Gordon MacRae, Richard Chamberlain, Yul Brenner, Michel Legrand, Frank Sinatra, Eddy Fisher, Charles Aznavour, Liberace, Henry Mancini, Jerry Orbach, Michael Feinstein, Rosemary Clooney, John McDermott, Peter Nero, Colm Wilkinson, Nathan Lane, Kevin Cole, Myron Cohen, Don Rickles, Sarah McLaughlin, Kenny G., Victor Borge, Shecky Green, Jack Jones, Pierce Brosnan, David Letterman, Barbara Cook, Robert Preston, David Foster, Terry Fox, Pamela Anderson.

If you prefer, just think of people you have encountered in your life. They don't need to be famous, but it is better and more effective than counting sheep. For example, if you attend a party or a function, try to remember who was there. What happens is that your mind becomes preoccupied with the project and you eventually fall asleep, usually sooner than later. Worth a try!

Committee: a group of men who individually can do nothing but as a group decide that nothing can be done.

SMART ISN'T ALWAYS SMART

I woke up, cheerfully, full of anticipation for my first day of school. It was my sixth birthday.

Grade 1 was easy for me. And then, half-way through Grade 2, my teacher recommended to my parents that I be advanced to Grade 3. They did so, and my marks for this advanced grade were more than satisfactory. And so, life for me in Grades 4 through 8 were challenging but produced outstanding marks. I finished either in first or second place scholastically during this time.

High school then beckoned. The school provided Grades 9 through 12 classes in the matriculation category. However, by mid-term in Grade 9, my marks were high enough for me to qualify for the three-year high school course that was available at the time. I took the advanced classes and thus completed high school in three years instead of the usual four.

The result of all the above was that, at the time of graduation, I was only fifteen years old (my birthday was coming up in September).

I hadn't made the right decisions! High school is not just a book learning institution but also an excellent exercise in human, social and personal interactions. Most of my contemporaries were two or three years older. As a result, important school programs such as sports, student councils and social activities, etc. were not practicable for me. I belatedly realized that it would have been far better for me not to have skipped a grade in primary school and not avail myself of the three-year course in high school. The result would have been far better social interactions with students of my own age.

YOU SEE, SMART ISN'T ALWAYS SMART!!

Change is not always better, but better is always a change.

HAND-EYE CO-ORDINATION

We often hear commentators on TV mention what wonderful hand-eye co-ordination some athletes have. A good example is the description of a hockey player knocking the puck out of mid air, probably into the net, which, it is thought, requires great hand-eye co-ordination.

Here's another point of view.

There is no question that knocking the puck out of mid air requires good hand-eye co-ordination. But it's not necessarily as great as the media would have us believe. In a baseball game, a batter faces a pitcher who is throwing a ball from 60 ft., 6 in. away, at 90 or more miles per hour. It takes excellent hand-eye co-ordination to hit the ball, and the batters are often successful. That is when great hand-eye co-ordination is really needed. A puck in mid-air does not compare!

The large print giveth and the small print taketh away!

BUSINESS SUGGESTIONS AND IDEAS

Suggestions and ideas from staff? Don't reject them because you think there's something wrong with them. There's something wrong with most good ideas but they should never be rejected until they are fully investigated.

Rejecting an idea so that you can get credit for a different one is not wise. Don't let your ego get in the way. Also, the idea might appear to be impossible at first but that isn't always the case. Be patient and don't decide too quickly.

If it appears to be illegal, wait a bit. The law in question could be changed.

Surround yourself with strong, successful people. They will provide you with the support you need when a good idea comes along, even if you have neither the time nor the resources to pursue it.

Remember that everyone doesn't always agree on the value of an idea. Good ones are often controversial and shouldn't be discarded too quickly.

Don't hesitate to embrace an idea even if it doesn't fit in your present modus operandi. Be flexible and don't be afraid to compromise.

Take risks, but calculated ones. If it succeeds, it will be worth it.

Take responsibility. Respect yourself and others as well.

Be generous with praise and cautious with criticism.

ONE DAY AT A TIME – LIFE IS A PRIVILEGE

This is an excerpt from a book entitled Living the Gift *by Charles E. Bower. He is (was) a Nova Scotian who documented the last days of his life as he died of Amyotrophic Lateral Sclerosis (ALS).*

Back in the '80s my friend was married to a woman who was afflicted with ALS. Through him I followed her journey up to the point where she could only blink her left eyelid. She soon died. A few years later, he remarried and shortly thereafter his new wife also became afflicted with ALS and I followed that journey. I can remember clearly thinking that that is one disease I really hope I don't end up with.

When I was first diagnosed with ALS, it seemed clear that I would take the off ramp before I became a quadriplegic. I could not imagine living in that condition, and yet here I am. Every day something is taken from my ability. It is not noticeable by the day but, like hair and fingernails, it adds up over a month. I have become entombed in a body, unable to do anything for myself. It's not my intention to complain (maybe a little bit). I simply want to report my experience of dying from ALS from the front lines.

I can tell you that without acceptance it would be so much tougher. Without acceptance, I would be a victim, a low-energy state comprised of guilt, blame, grief, regret, fear, anxiety, disappointment, anger and aggression. I choose not to be a victim. I choose to accept reality. I add to that reality generous amounts of gratitude for being born into this incredible opportunity called life, into this adventure, into this movie. I'm so very, very grateful to have the ability to explore my life while embracing my death, going day after day deeper into the recesses of my mind, coming to see all of the connections and patterns in my life, and reconnecting with my teachers. Fire was a teacher for me. Pauline, my friends, my family, daily life itself are the teachers, and of course the greatest teacher of all has been…experience.

Every day the noose tightens ever so slightly, the trapdoor groans under my weight. I labour more and more for each breath. I spend my time not so much on the mystery of death but on an even more profound mystery — life. What I know is I am very, very blessed, lucky and fortunate. I was born in Canada, my parents did their best, and I felt safe. My genetics are excellent, and I had some mysterious processes that protected me. There's no doubt that if they exist, I had a guardian angel. I am very happy and content with the life I have experienced, the friends

I have encountered and my worldly adventures. I'm thankful in the extreme for the dozens and dozens of personal development workshops I have attended. I had a body that worked exquisitely well for seventy years. Some people believe that wealth is money, which is partially true. I found that one of my greatest sources of wealth was free time, of which I had lots and lots. I've been with a woman that loves me for almost forty years. I helped raise four children who are all contributing members of society. I have experienced the thrill of victory and the agony of defeat…I lived a life of privilege.

In this, my time of dying, there seems to be so many mysteries, so many questions and so few answers.

One of the questions I wrestle with is why, at this incredible feast called life, did I show up sometimes with such a little spoon? Why did I sometimes settle for crumbs? Now that I have passed through the gate of no return, I can look over the fence and see you on the other side. With a bullhorn, I ask, "Where are you in your relationships, your dreams, your desires? Where in your life have you fallen asleep?" And with the volume at full, I say, "Wake up, wake up! You will have lots of time to sleep when you're dead." In the feast of life, are you getting what you need?

The size of the audience is not important. Do your best anyway.

UNINTENDED SEXISM

Tom greets Helen as she enters the room. She is using a walker, a particularly good model.

He says, "The guy that invented that walker sure did the world a big favour."

Helen replied, "A guy??"

You only get one chance to make a first impression.

TOP TEN SONGS LIST

A website on the internet recently released a list of what they considered to be the fifty best songs ever recorded based on record sales. This list includes many various tastes in music. For your information, the Beatles are the performers mentioned most often in the list.

Here are the top ten!

10. *Thriller* - Michael Jackson

9. *Good Vibrations* - The Beach Boys

8. *My Way* - Frank Sinatra

7. *Sexual Healing* - Marvin Gaye

6. *Comfortably Numb* - Pink Floyd

5. *Wonderwall* - Oasis

4. *Piano Man* - Billy Joel

3. *Dreams* - Fleetwood Mac

2. *Superstition* - Stevie Wonder

1. *Bohemian Rhapsody* - Queen

Lots of room for discussion and controversy in this list but it is an interesting exercise and the list can provoke many an argument.

HERE ARE MY TOP TEN FAVOURITES

Jogging Along - John Arpin
Finale, 1st Act, *Les Misérables* original cast.
Lily's Eyes - Original cast recording of *The Secret Garden*
My Way - Frank Sinatra
You Needed Me - Anne Murray
La Bohème - Charles Aznavour
Chances Are - Johnny Mathis
Perhaps Love - John Denver and Placido Domingo
Chopsticks - Liberace
I Dreamed a Dream - Susan Boyle

"There are good days and there are bad days, and this is one of them." - Lawrence Welk

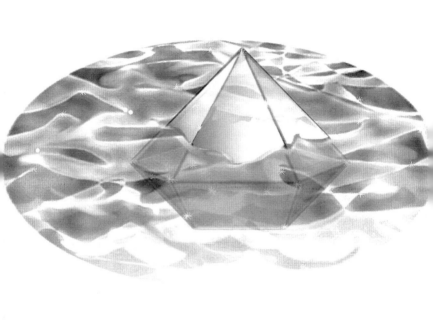

THE JEWEL OF THE SONGHEES - INTRO

Victoria is the capital of Canada's most westerly province, British Columbia. It has a population of 96,000. It has moved on from its traditional description of it being a city that was "For the newlyweds or the nearly deads." It now has a thriving business community and is considered one of the top "tech" cities in Canada. It has the best all around weather in the country and, despite its high cost of living, is a treasured location for Canadians living.

One of the charming areas in Victoria is the Songhees Walkway that is located on the north side of the harbour. It is a favourite of walkers who take advantage of it year-round. The following poem is a tribute to this area from a long-time user of this wonderful facility.

Tourist question: Is that the same moon we get in Texas?

THE JEWEL OF
THE SONGHEES

I often stroll the West Bay walk, to breathe the air there, have a talk
With friends who love this magic place, they too, its wonders they embrace.
It never ceases to impress; it holds a certain timelessness.
The ambience that we hold dear, provides a montage far and near.
Silver on water atmosphere that disappears then reappears.

The kayaks, planes, the Coho too, which suddenly comes into view
Appear from nowhere, like a dream, with little effort so it seems.
And little ferry boats are there, they'll take you almost anywhere.

The herons stand so deathly still, until they hone in for the kill
Of helpless fish, that we can't see, 'til in their beaks, quite visibly
Appear their prey, so motionless, their lives are done, no more distress.

The cosmos, here, is everywhere with ducks and geese beyond compare.
And whale boats pass by every hour with tourists seeking to see our
Beasts of the sea, the Orca ones, they live in pods and all these runs
Provide a spectacle at sea, that folks from far come here to see
The grandeur of these animals, that really are majestic.

A famous pub is on this route, its reputation absolute.
A world class hotel's here as well, it hosts some well-known clientele.
A new marina joined the scene, the price of yachts there — quite obscene.
But folks who own them, we've no doubt, spend real money when they're about.

Along the way, and at no fee, several benches face out to sea.
Folks stop to read their papers there, sip some tea or breathe in the air.

Look to the south, and you will see, cruise ships arriving, sometimes three.
And further south, the USA. Our friendly neighbours, awesome eh?

To cover all the many things, the highlights worth remembering
The many facets of this walk, it's face to face we'd need to talk.
It symbolizes who we are, why tourists come, by boat, by car
To saunter down this pretty route, it's ecstasy is absolute.
These people feel euphoria, when they come to Victoria.

RGL

Nobody can make you happy until you are happy with yourself first.

THE GAUDET NAME AND THE EXPULSION OF THE ACADIANS

I was born in Moncton, NB, which is the home of many Acadians. My mother, her mother and her mother's mother were all Gaudets. To this day, especially in Southern New Brunswick and Prince Edward Island, there are many inhabitants called Gaudet. Their name is pronounced "God -ets" or something similar. Many familiar names have Acadia as its origin. For example, Cormier, Leger, Arsenault, LeBlanc, Melanson, Gauvin, Surette, Poirier, Savoie, Chiasson, Landry, and Richard are some of the more common names whose roots are Acadian.

Here in British Columbia where I now reside, the name Gaudet takes on a new pronunciation. It is often pronounced "Goodie." I have no idea why there is this change of pronunciation out here in the west. Over the years, there have been many alterations in spelling of the surname Gaudet. Some of the spelling variations include, Gaudette, Gaudait, Gaudies, Gaudey, Godet, Godette, Godait, Godais, Goday, Goddet, Goddette and many more.

The Gaudet name originated as far back as 1340 in Normandy, France. By the year 1675, there were 500 Acadians in Nova Scotia that had migrated from France. The Acadians first settled in Nova Scotia in 1604. In the treaty of Utrecht, the Acadians were ceded by France to Britain in 1713.

In 1755, 10,000 French Acadians refused to take an oath of allegiance to England. The new governor, Charles Lawrence, was not the conciliator that the previous governor had been. As a result, all the Acadians were deported and their lands and possessions confiscated. Many, if not most, were separated from their families and loved ones. Some found refuge as far away as Louisiana (thus the term Cajuns); Galveston, Texas; Baltimore, Maryland; Ellis Island, New York; Boston, Massachusetts; Connecticut and various other regions of the USA as well as parts of New Brunswick and Cape Breton Island. Some ventured as far as France and the Caribbean.

Between 1755 and 1763, there were 7000 French in Quebec (then known as New France). Here, the French people flourished, founding Lower Canada, one of the two great solitudes that became Canada. Many of the Gaudets of the era were prominent in social, cultural, religious and political affairs in New France. Thus, the beginning of the area now known as the province of Quebec.

It has been my privilege to visit Grand Pre on several occasions. The expulsion is duly highlighted in the area. The original church still stands and regular performances of a play that depicts the story of the deportation is presented daily.

Plan your life like you will live forever, and live your life like you will die the next day.

AN EMBARRASSING MOMENT

One evening, four of us set out for dinner and a movie. The dinner was most pleasant and we then proceeded to the theatre. When we arrived there, I felt my back pocket and said, "I left my wallet at the restaurant." My friends suggested we return there immediately but I nixed the idea saying that they knew me at the restaurant because I'd been there several times, and so I suggested we look for my wallet after the movie.

At the restaurant after the movie, I asked the manager if a wallet had been found. He asked me what it looked like. From force of habit I suppose, my hand went to my back pocket and lo and behold the wallet was there. I told him that the wallet looked just like the one I produced from my back pocket! Boy, was I embarrassed!!

Apparently, the back pocket on the pants I was wearing was particularly deep so that when I felt for my wallet at the theatre, I presume that I felt the top of the pocket and, of course, there was nothing there. Had I felt a little farther down in the pocket,

I would have realized that the wallet was, in fact, exactly where I thought it was.

My friends had a good laugh at my expense and I resolved that, in future, I would double-check my pocket before assuming that my wallet wasn't there.

If I had a dollar for every girl that found me unattractive, they'd eventually find me very attractive.

HIS NAME WAS KATOU

I was born and raised in Moncton, New Brunswick. Occasionally, a friend of mine who still lives there sends me clippings from the *Moncton Transcript*. They are usually about sports events in that city, since both of us were very much involved in the sports scene when I lived there. He still is, so the articles he sends usually have some connection or other to our past mutual interests.

Yesterday, I received another of his clippings. This time is was a full page of the paper that referred to the recent CFL game that was played in Moncton. The city is trying hard to attract a CFL franchise and the sold out stadium at this particular game could go a long way to making this happen.

I happened to turn the page over to see what was on the other side. Interestingly enough, it was a page of obituaries. I took particular note of the one for Mr. Lawrence Cormier. When I was in primary school, I knew him as Katou — he was the school bully par excellence.

Although I am now six feet tall, back when I was in Grade 6, I was the smallest guy in the school — the runt of the litter. Since I always had high marks and often led the class scholastically, Katou took great pleasure in picking on me, almost daily, with punches to both my arms. I recalled those unpleasant times while I was reading his obituary. I had often wondered what had happened to him. One friend thought he had ended up in prison. If that was the case, I would not have been surprised.

Knowing that he was now dead, I thought I might feel a certain feeling of elation or revenge. I felt nothing.

The short fortune teller who escaped from prison was a small medium at large.

A NOVA SCOTIA MYSTERY

Mr. Alex Jones takes a flight from the Los Angeles International Airport to Boston's Logan International Airport, then to Halifax International Airport, arriving on the 5:00 p.m. flight. He then rents a car from Hertz and drives through the Annapolis Valley of Nova Scotia to a very secluded business training facility called Highland, located approximately 110 miles west of Halifax. He is there to attend a top secret seminar of twenty world-renowned scientists who are working on a joint project aimed at eliminating electricity and gasoline in the world by means of the use of solar and oxygen energy combined with water.

The eighteen men and two women who are attending this meeting are from all over the globe including Canada, the United States, Russia, France, Germany and England to name a few. The meeting has been convened by the Canadian Department of Science and Technology, after learning that noted scientist Emile LaTourenne of France is strongly rumoured to have made a new top secret discovery in his field that will revolutionize the use of electricity and fossil fuels in the world.

Because the effect such a discovery would have on the industrial world, particularly on those companies active in the fields of automobiles and electricity, major security precautions have been put in place. The need for secrecy regarding the actual meeting is of the highest priority. RCMP Chief of Detectives Charles Bowen, world-renowned for his uncanny ability to provide top notch security support and for his extraordinary skill in the questioning of suspects, has been assigned to be the man on the scene. His cover is that he is the owner and managing director of Highland.

Highly skilled and top-security-cleared translators on loan from the United Nations are present to facilitate meaningful communications among the delegates. It is to be a three-day meeting, with three-hour sessions each morning and afternoon, and a relaxing, more social atmosphere prevailing in the evenings. Paula Bowen, wife of Charles Bowen, is responsible for the social aspects of the event. She is also presented as the principal teacher/leader of the many courses that are available at Highland.

None of the delegates are known to each other, except by reputation. The roster of the delegates was compiled by the Department of Development and Research of the United Nations whose director in chief, Diane Daley, will be chairing the sessions. All are meeting each other for the first time. The first session is to start at 9:00 a.m., but Charles

Bowen has noted that Emile LaTourenne has yet to make an appearance. After waiting twenty minutes, Mr. Bowen decides to check up on him and proceeds to his room.

Finding the door ajar, he enters and much to his horror finds Mr. LaTourenne on the floor, dead. His throat has been slashed and there is considerable blood everywhere. Bowen decides not to immediately advise the others in order to give him some time to assess the situation. He calls on Diane to convene the meeting, who then calls on Paula Bowen to lead the group in one of the regular Highland programs as a way to keep the delegates occupied. Paula announces, without explanation, that the intended seminars would begin that afternoon. The agenda for the morning sessions will consist of personal group studies focusing on the Myers-Briggs Type Indicator program. All attendees received the Myers-Briggs test in advance and the results were forwarded to event organizers for analysis. These tests are renowned for their ability to identify the likes, tendencies and preferences of anyone taking the test. Charles Bowen has access to these results. He believes that any knowledge of each individual could assist him.

The delegates are divided into two groups and each group is asked to retire to separate rooms, which are off the main seminar room. They are then asked to decide, as a group, what would be the ideal vacation if money was no object. What the participants are not aware of, is that the results of the Myers-Briggs test clearly indicated that some individuals were extroverts, and some were introverts. The two groups were divided using these personal tendencies. One group was exclusively introverts and the other group all extroverts. Each group was then asked, after thirty minutes of deliberations, to tell everyone assembled what they decided was an ideal vacation.

The results were amusing and eye-opening, if not predictable.

Introverts - Plans were suggested for various trips for such solo activities as fishing, reading, hiking and other solo enterprises.

Extroverts - It would never occur to any of the extroverts to plan something that didn't include the whole group. Accordingly, fancy trips to New York's Broadway or cruises to various parts of the world were the norm.

Each participant was part of the group report and it was not difficult to ascertain who were the extroverts and who were the introverts.

Paul Bowen immediately realized that the test results of one Alex Jones clearly indicated that he was an introvert, and a strong one at that. There was no doubt that, based on his performance in the vacations grouping, Alex Jones came across as a very strong extrovert thus causing Paul Bowen to take him aside for questioning

Using his considerable skills, Bowen quickly discovered that Alex Jones was indeed an impostor. He had been commandeered to attend the seminar. His first step was to eliminate the real Alex Jones and take his place. His second step was to assassinate Emile LaTourenne. Jones was hired by a consortium of executives of large corporations who did not want LaTourenne's discoveries made available to the world and thus hamper the progress of the corporations that they represented.

Thankfully, LaTourenne had confided his findings in his assistant who joined the group the next day and the sessions proceeded as originally planned. LaTourenne's scientific work was only in its infancy stage and would need considerable additional research for his project to become a reality. The sessions at Highland proved to be informative to LaTourenne's team, and they left Highland with a renewed sense of purpose and dedication.

The fatality of good resolutions is that they are always too late.

INTERESTING THOUGHTS

Why do kamikaze pilots wear helmets?

- Dave Edison

If you're caught on a golf course during a thunderstorm and are afraid of lightning, hold up a one iron. Not even God can hit a one iron.

- Lee Trevino

The people who gave us golf and called it a game are the same people who gave us bagpipes and called it music.

- Source unknown

I bet on a horse that went off at ten to one. He finished at two thirty and came in last.

- Henny Youngman

You know you're getting old when everything hurts. And what doesn't hurt doesn't work.

- Hy Gardner

I stopped believing in Santa Claus when I was six. My mother took me to see him in a department store and he asked me for my autograph.

- Shirley Temple

I have often wanted to drown my troubles, but I can't get my wife to go swimming.

- Jimmy Carter

Lady Astor to Winston Churchill. "Sir you are drunk." Churchill's reply: "Yes madam, and you are ugly. But in the morning, I will be sober and you will still be ugly."

Politicians and diapers have one thing in common. They should be changed regularly, and for the same reason. - Author unknown

If 2/2/22 falls on a Tuesday, we'll just call it "2s Day." (It does fall on a Tuesday).

Why is the letter W, in English, called double U? Shouldn't it be called double V?

Every time you clean something, you just make something else dirty.

The only thing that is worse than a quitter is the man who is afraid to begin.

RESTAURANT ADVENTURES

A few years ago, my wife and I joined another couple for dinner at a restaurant here in Victoria. When asked if they had Diet Coke without caffeine, they replied that they didn't. We enjoyed our meal and resolved to visit this restaurant again at some future date.

I cannot handle caffeine in the evening as it keeps me awake. Thus, on our second visit to this restaurant, this time in the evening, I brought a can of Diet Coke without caffeine, which my wife held in her purse. When our waiter came to take our order, I asked, out of courtesy I thought, if it was OK to use the Diet Coke. Our waiter said he would inquire and when he returned, he advised that management had a policy of no outside drinks allowed. Presumably this was aimed at people bringing in their own liquor. I advised the waiter that the can of Coke was unopened, but still the decision stood. We left the restaurant and never returned and neither did the couple who originally introduced us to that venue.

That restaurant is now out of business. No small wonder!

On another occasion, we planned to entertain an out of town visitor with a night out at a nearby restaurant. Once we were properly seated, our visitor, an eighty-two-year-old lady, had difficulty understanding the conversation, as did we, because the background music was quite loud. We asked our waiter if it was possible to lower the volume of the music, and he said he would check. When he returned, he advised us that it was the policy of management to play the music at that level and that it would not be adjusted.

We left the restaurant and spent over $100 in a nearby establishment where the background music was much more tolerable.

That restaurant is now out of business.

Stupidity is not a crime but it should be.

POUTINE

In British Columbia at least, poutine is a dish that includes French fries and cheese curds topped with a brown gravy. It originated in the province of Quebec in the late 1950s and has long been associated with Quebec cuisine.

However, in Atlantic Canada, especially in "Acadia," (which is generally known as the southern part of New Brunswick and a large part of Nova Scotia), the term "poutine" means something totally different.

Poutines were known as Poutine Rapees by the Acadians. It is a potato dumpling dish with a mixture of seasoned pork in the centre. It is usually prepared with a mixture of grated and mashed potatoes. It is considered a national dish. The greyish colour and gluey texture of the poutines make them appear somewhat unappetizing. Their taste more than compensates for their unattractive appearance and is a great favourite for all Acadians who enjoyed this delicacy, usually at Mardi Gras time, just before lent.

If it works, it's out of date.

GETTING TO CARNEGIE HALL

There's an old joke that says, "How Do You Get to Carnegie Hall?" The answer of course was "practice, practice, practice." That is undoubtedly true for musicians. However, my experience was quite different.

Several years ago, I lived in Halifax and was on the Board of Directors of the Nova Scotia Symphony. I was planning a motor trip to New York City and, since the symphony was at that time having serious discussions about the Pops programming, I suggested that a call be made to the offices of the New York Pops, in order to arrange an appointment for me with the Promotions Director of their orchestra. The purpose of my meeting with this individual was to learn more about the planning and structuring of Pops concerts.

The meeting took place in the offices of the Director, and provided useful information which I passed on to the board in Halifax. It turned out that the man's offices were located in the same building as Carnegie Hall.

When our meeting concluded, I asked if it were possible for me to see the famous Hall. I was told "of course". A closed door was pointed out and I was directed to simply go through it. I did so and found myself on the stage of Carnegie Hall. The Hall was empty of course but the thrill of seeing it and actually standing on the stage of this great Hall was a moment to be remembered.

A man knocked on my door and asked for a small donation towards the local swimming pool, so I gave him a glass of water.

EPILOGUE

Thank you for journeying through my book. I hope you had a few chuckles along the way as well as enjoying the "touchy-feely" stories contained herein.

You may have observed that there are no Trump jokes included in this book. I have, over the years, attempted to stay away from that subject but, unfortunately, I cannot in clear conscience close out this book of levity and compassion without including one that has been with me for some time.

It appears that there has been a sandwich named after Mr. Trump. It includes two slices of bread, white of course, covered with a special Russian sauce and containing — wait for it — lots of baloney.

Thanks again for your participation. If the book made your day just a little lighter and more joyful, then I have accomplished what I set out to do.

Bob LeBlanc

MEET THE AUTHOR

I am a fluently bilingual Acadian, born in Moncton N.B. where I graduated from high school and then completed a business college course in typing and shorthand.

I pursued many sports activities especially in hockey where I attained the senior level in hockey as a goalie. I have lived in Moncton (of course), Halifax, Bridgewater, Montreal, Quebec City and London, ON. I presently reside in Victoria, B.C.

I have been a Regional Manager in finance in both New Brunswick and the Province of Quebec. I subsequently was a publisher in Halifax for 12 years before moving to Victoria.

I have four grown children and am very proud of all of them. They have all succeeded in life.

As a successful businessman, I have had varied careers in Finance, Car Rentals and Publishing ending my career in a franchise operation called FastSigns here in Victoria.

Besides pursuing a career as a writer, even at the late stages of my life (85), I have participated in several musical enterprises both in Halifax and in Victoria. I founded the singing group Variety Fare, which performed in both Halifax and Victoria, and the Victoria Broadway Chorus, as well as the Dinner Theatres at both the old and the new Oak Bay Beach Hotels as well as the Ambrosia Dinner Theatre. I am a pianist and still entertain at several Seniors" homes in Victoria. (i.e. Shannon Oaks Retirement Home and Parkwood Place among others).

This book has been a project on the back burner for some time and it is particularly satisfying to finally see my ideas in print.